Treating your
Husband
as a
King

KINGSLEY
APPIAGYEI

Unless otherwise indicated, all scripture quotations are from the New King James Version of the Bible.

TREATING YOUR HUSBAND AS A KING
ISBN 978-0-9565983-1-8
Copyright © 2010 by KINGSLEY APPIAGYEI

Published by:
Kings House Publishing
2 Thornlaw Road
London
SE27 0SA
Email: kingshouse@sky.com

DEDICATION

To my family – for loving me, for encouraging me
and for always being there.
To all who desire to enhance their relationship so that
their homes become a mini kingdom of kings and
queens, princes and princesses.

To the source of all knowledge and wisdom,
my Lord and Saviour Jesus Christ.

CONTENTS

INTRODUCTION

I believe that the major reason why many marriages are struggling in our day is simply because couples do not make a quality decision to commit fully to Christ. Jesus says:

"I am the vine and you are the branches – he who abides in me, and I in him, bears much fruit for without me you can do nothing"

The abiding believer is a legitimate believer. Your fruitfulness is dependent on abiding in Christ. In 2 Peter 1:10, Peter the Apostle in his letter to the churches in Asia Minor talks to them about fruitful growth in the faith. As he does that he continues in verse 10 with the following words:

"Brethren be even more diligent to make your call and election sure for if you do these things you will never stumble"

What this Scripture is teaching us is that we must make our call and election certain. How do we do that? By becoming diligent and by doing whatever it takes to make our calling worthwhile. For that reason, Peter in verses 11-13 says that he will not neglect his duty but will stir up the believers by reminding them of the truth they already know so that they will still hold on to the truth even after he has departed.

A FRUITFUL MARRIAGE

I strongly believe that one of the major reasons why many marriages are struggling is simply because they have not made Jesus Christ the centre of their marriages. The truth about life is that until Jesus becomes the centre of the marriage relationship, it will struggle. In John 15:5 Jesus himself says:

"I am the vine and you are the branches. He who abides in me and I in him bears much fruit, for without me you can do nothing"

In other words Jesus makes it quite clear that he has called us to bear fruit – He has put couples together to be fruitful. However unless we remain connected to the vine, fruitfulness will elude us.

May your marriage become fruitful and bear the fruit of peace even as you stay close to the vine. May He who is the Sweet Rose of Sharon bring fragrance back into your relationship. My prayer is that Psalm 1 will become a reality in your life as you abide in Him. You will become like a tree planted by the waters and you will bring forth your fruit in season!

Your marriage will bear fruit and your leaf shall not wither in the name of Jesus. Divorce will not rear its head in your marriage because you will stay close to the vine, and whatever you do shall prosper.

Marriages that are planted on the rock – that is Jesus – will stand. They will not be shaky because Jesus is our firm foundation. May health be the portion of your family in the Name of Jesus. It is my prayer that God will not only lift your marriage and plant it on the rock to stay, but much more, it will become a living epistle and a testimony among your family and friends. May you accomplish this through your fruit-bearing life-style.

Treating your husband as a King is birthed from a desire to see Christians fulfilled in their marriages. My experience is that marriage hinges on everything we do. If a marriage is sound, then the partners in that marriage flourish in every aspect of their lives. My aim of writing this book is to help you understand how the treatment you give to your husband can in fact make him feel like a royal; indeed we are supposed to be kings and queens in our own homes. Treating each other in this manner certainly creates an atmosphere where the Lord reigns. It brings favour and sanity and creates a peaceful nest where children can flourish.

As you read this book, my prayer is that your marriage will become fruitful and bear the fruit of peace, because He is the Prince of Peace, and as the Sweet Rose of Sharon, may His fragrance fill your marriage. May you be like a tree planted by rivers of living water, and may you prosper in whatever you do. As you read, ask the Lord for the grace to work on any unhelpful attitudes He may highlight. May Jesus become real in your marriage, and may your home blossom like a beautiful flower in the name of Jesus. May the grace that brings salvation cause your marriage and family to prosper in your generation. Amen.

CHAPTER 1

QUESTIONS MEN ASK ABOUT WOMEN

It is important to note that men are different from women in a lot of ways. Sometimes men are at a loss as to why their wives think or behave in a certain way. The differences are quite fascinating, and it is essential that you know some of the questions men ask about women. These are some of them:

Why are women so emotional?

They weep when they should not weep, and they laugh when you do not expect them to laugh. Women are naturally made to express their feelings more than men.

Why do women spend so much time on how they look?

If our ladies would spend the same amount of time, even half the amount of time they spend on their make-up in prayer, all our prayer requests would be answered!

How come she talks so much and does not get tired?

Wives need to understand that as much as one of their major needs is for husbands to communicate with them, it is also important to recognise that men sometimes just want to be quiet. Wives need to work out the right balance, where he will talk to you when you want to talk, and you will in turn give him the freedom to remain quiet when he wants to do so. In my book *"Treating your wife as a queen"*, I admonish husbands to initiate communication sometimes.

Why can't she let things go?

Women are such that they can remember things that happened twenty, even thirty years ago. They are like "archaeologists", digging up the past. She could say to the husband: "Five years ago you did the same thing" and most often the man is at a loss because he cannot remember that he did that.

There are too many hurting people in the Church of Jesus Christ. This comes about because for many of us when we said "yes" to Jesus, we did not die to self. You see, dead men cannot feel pain; dead men cannot be hurt – and the truth is that you and I are *"crucified with Christ"*. The life we live now, we live by faith, through the Son of God who loved us and died for us. (Galatians 2:20) This implies that our old nature must die. What God expects of you is that you die to self so that when you hear unpleasant things being said about you, you can ask for the grace to forgive, let go and move on.

Why do they work so hard on relationships?

Women work on their relationships because by their very nature, they are relational, therefore their environment is part of their life. Men on the other hand are the opposite.

In regards to this subject, wives need to understand the background to their husbands' early relationships, especially with their parents or guardians. Some men may have travelled many paths which may have combined to make them who they are. Some men had a very tough upbringing; some grew up not knowing who their dads were. Many have also grown up not experiencing the comfort of a home where the father demonstrated godly headship. The truth about men is that they are unable to deal with the lack of parental care. However, women are somewhat different. Girls by nature have something built within them that make them natural mothers and nurturers. Men on the other hand need that support from their wives.

T.D. Jakes holds several meetings for men every year and at one of such "Manpower" meetings, he spoke about men who had grown up without fathers. In his invitation after the preaching, he gave an altar call for people to come forward for prayer and it was shocking to see the number of men who went forward, some weeping like boys. For many of such men, as they look back at their childhood days, the pain of not having had a good relationship with their fathers is something they find hard to wrestle with. The place of a wife in such a man's life is to be his helpmeet. If you are the wife of such a man, you will need to do everything to assure him that you will be more than a hundred fathers to him! God has placed you in his life so that you will encourage, and support him in every way you can. Be a pillar on which he can lean, so that the hurts and pain due to past relationships with family or other, would only become shadows in his life. You have what it takes to do this.

Men put so much confidence in their wives, hence use your God-given abilities, your character and the power of your womanhood to strengthen and encourage your husband and let him know you are there for him.

The above are just a few of the areas where women are different from men. These should not be a cause for misunderstanding between couples, as they highlight the different and unique ways God has wired the opposite sexes. It is important that we give some thought to this aspect of differences in dealing with relationships, especially in the context of marriage.

To treat your husband as a king, one needs to find out what makes a husband fulfilled. However, it is not enough to know these. One has to go the extra mile to work on them. In the chapters that follow, I address:

- The power of submission and respect

- Fulfilling his "No.1" need

- The significance of making yourself attractive for him,

- The value of home management and support

- The importance of affirmation and admiration

CHAPTER 2

THE POWER OF SUBMISSION AND RESPECT

A principle which has become a big problem for many people, especially women, is "submission". As we look at the practical ways of how to treat your husband as a king, I will focus on the wife's function of submission. There is a Spanish proverb which says *"woe to the house where the hen crows and the cock keeps quiet"*! You and I know very well that a hen is not made to crow. So if the hen is crowing in your house, something is certainly wrong! This proverb means that someone has to be in charge, but it better be the one that God has designed for the task.

Roles determine relationships

For instance, in a ship where there is more than one captain, there is the risk that each may give different or conflicting instructions. In a home where the roles are clearly defined, understood and acted upon, that home will certainly blossom.

Unfortunately, the concept of many men when it comes to headship and authority in the home, comes largely from the natural mind and not from a careful study of Scripture. To them they have only experienced a pattern in their own homes when they were growing up – a pattern where perhaps, their dad never allowed their mum to have any say in the life of the family and so their concept of headship is about men who only know how to use women. The truth is that many of us have grown up having a wrong concept of submission. It is my prayer that the Lord will help us understand it the way He intended it, for there is power in exercising submission.

The two are equal but have different functions

The question many ask is this: "If a husband is appointed by God to be the leader in a marriage, does that mean that he is regarded as the sole superior partner?" The Bible tells us that husband and wife are equal in the sight of God. 1 Peter 3:7 says *"Together we are heirs of the grace of life"*. The two are equal, however, they have different functions. It is very important that we understand this.

A husband and wife are equal spiritually. However, the admonition to **Love** and **Submit** are functional differences established by God and any attempt to change this will only lead to disaster. This does not mean that women are only to submit without loving their husbands. In several instances in Scripture, we are admonished to love and submit to God, and to one another. For example:

Ephesians 5:21:

"Submitting yourselves one to another in the fear of God"

James 4:7:

Submit yourselves therefore to God..."

1 Peter 2:17:

> *"Show proper respect to everyone. Love the brotherhood of*
> *believers, fear God, honour the king"*

Therefore, if you are already exercising love and submission towards God and towards one another, for example in the context of your Church community with your Christian brothers and sisters, or at your workplace, then it should not be a big deal to function in these roles in our marriage relationship as God intends it. The closest person to you, apart from God is your spouse, hence they should be the first to enjoy the expressions of love and submission in the marriage context!

In Galatians 3:28 Paul says:

> *"There is neither Jew nor Greek, there is neither bond nor free,*
> *there is neither male nor female: for you are all one in Christ*
> *Jesus."*

Paul here is talking about people's individual worth. Although he is not talking primarily about marriage, the verse highlights the fact that God sees male and female as equal. **Submission is therefore to be seen as God sees it**. It is an instruction given by God to women to help bring harmony in the home, and God does not intend it to mean that they are inferior or second-rate by any means.

The truth, however, is that many women struggle with submission. One woman once said to me, "Pastor, I do not mind if my husband says he is the head. I will let him be the head, and I will be the neck. As long as I am turning the head I do not mind". Unfortunately, that is what many wives do, but that is far from what God intends it.

Submission, when exercised with understanding is not something to be feared, but to be enjoyed.

What Submission is not

Submission does not mean that the wife should become passive. It is not about a woman giving up her passions, dreams, opinions or her identity to please her husband. Submission does not mean a wife should tolerate abuse. If as a wife you are having to deal with a husband's physical, verbal or emotional abuse, you must seek help. Submission does not mean that you become a punching bag for your husband! Any form of violent or abnormal behaviour must caution such a woman to seek help because that is ungodly. The Lord's expectation of the command to the man to love you requires that you are protected.

What then is Submission?

Submission is the act of yielding to the authority and headship of your husband by an act of your will, without compulsion. It is acknowledging his leadership as instituted by God and joyfully letting him lead the marriage union even though at times you may not totally agree on everything.

Submission is really an attitude or frame of mind and it must be voluntary. It recognises that just as Christ is submissive to God and the Church is subject to Christ, so a wife ought to be submissive to her own husband. The Bible states in Philippians 2:4:

> "Jesus, even though He was God, did not consider equality with God to be grasped, but took upon Himself the form of a servant becoming obedient to death, even death on a cross"

In other words, Jesus humbled Himself and subjected Himself under the headship of God. No Church will survive if Christ is not the head of that Church. So the Bible is saying that just as Christ subjected Himself to God and the Church subjects itself to God, in like manner, the woman must submit herself under the leadership of her husband. Submission means humble obedience to the husband.

The issue of submission is central to God's heart, and that is why he emphasises it over and over again. Submission does not mean that the husband should walk over his wife like a doormat. In fact, any husband who genuinely fears God will love his wife as Christ loved the Church. Any woman who submits naturally to the husband will also be blessed of the Lord, because she exhibits a life of obedience.

1 Peter 3:1-6

"Wives in the same way be submissive to your own husbands so that if any of them do not believe the word, they may be won over without words but by the behaviour of their wives when they see the purity and reverence of your lives. Your beauty should not come from outward adornment such as braided hair and the wearing of gold jewellery and fine clothes. Instead it should be that of your inner self, the unfading beauty of a quiet and gentle spirit which is of great worth in God's sight, for this is the way the holy women of old who put their hope in God used to make themselves beautiful. They were submissive to their own husbands like Sarah who obeyed Abraham and called him her master. You are her daughters if you do what is right and do not give way to fear."

The Lord says that wives are to submit. The command is unqualified, applying to every wife no matter her abilities, educational or social status; knowledge of Scripture or spiritual maturity. Let me explain this. Let's take the scenario of a woman who is a high court judge – what happens in court is that as soon as the judge enters, the court clerk announces to the court to rise and everybody stands up to acknowledge this lady judge. In that context, she is the head. However, when that woman returns home, all that ceases. At home, she is not the head, as she is in court. Today, there are many women in such high positions. They manage reputable companies and businesses and many have excelled in their careers, some becoming CEO's. That is very good, and I am all for women pursing their careers and doing very well. My caution though, to such women is that they become careful that the command they wield in their work places does not affect how they operate in their homes. My admonition to such women is that they submit to her own husbands at home. That is the wisdom of God. Note that until a woman submits, it will become very difficult for the man to lead.

It should be a "willing" submission

Wives, please note that the godly submission expected of a wife is not for the husband to command, but for the wife to willingly and lovingly offer. You are to voluntarily yield yourself under the headship of your husband. Godly submission ought to be an act of obedience and love for God and the man. The Bible describes how wives should do that:

> "Wives, submit yourself to your own husband as to the Lord"
> (Eph 5:22)

In other words, the key is for the wife to first submit to the Lord. It then becomes natural to submit to her husband. She submits to the man she possesses as her own. She submits as an act of obedience to the Lord who has given that command. You need to understand and note this well, that God sees your

20

submission to your husband as your obedience to Jesus Christ, because it is He that has given the command.

When a woman submits:

a) She acknowledges and demonstrates first and foremost, her obedience to God; and do not forget that obedience to God comes with a blessing.

b) She also acknowledges the fact that God has placed her husband over her to be her spiritual covering and protection, and that God seeks her interest and nothing else!

I believe that God has so ordered things this way, so that the woman is relieved of the stresses and strains of life because God has arranged and equipped the husband to bear all the battles that come over the family. As a wife responds to God's word and submits to her husband, she enjoys protection and fulfilment.

Be a woman who understands that your major role in the marriage is to submit voluntarily to your husband. Again, understand that your husband's major role is to be a prophet, priest and king in the marriage, and to diligently and passionately love you with all his heart, just as Jesus loved the church and sacrificially gave Himself for it.

In what ways are wives to submit?

In what ways do I submit to my husband, you may ask. These are some of the ways:

Let him have the final say

To submit to your husband, you ought to let him have the final say in matters. Transfer to him the responsibility of making final decisions. The truth is that women naturally have an intuition that eludes men. No wise man will seek to lead in areas where he is ignorant, whilst the wife has the expertise. You probably may be asking: "What if I sense his decision is wrong – do I still have to submit and just let him go ahead"? I suggest that the wife after sharing her views, leaves the final decision to her husband. However, politely ask for a delay in its execution while the two of you seek Godly counsel and pray. Wives need to understand the privilege of taking their case to a "higher court" through prayer. Proverbs 19:21 says:

> *"The heart of the king (and your husband is a king) is in the hands of the Lord"*

If you genuinely, in an act of submission, take the issue to God, He is able to speak to your husband in so many ways. A man will value your advice more highly if you are a loving and submissive wife. I do know that when it comes to intuition, usually the women cannot fully explain why it is that they are uncomfortable with certain decisions – they simply know they cannot flow with a decision, but cannot explain it. They would usually say "I don't feel comfortable with this". Understand ladies, that most men use speech to express ideas and communicate factual information, whereas women usually use speech to express feelings or vent their emotions. For that reason, make sure that when you do not agree with him, you ask God for the grace to take your time to explain to him why you do not agree with him. Do this calmly and clearly, dealing with the issues concerned.

You may ask: "so what do I do if my husband does not consult me for my opinion on important matters"? My suggestion is that you give your opinion anyway. Do that in a skilful and godly way, with so much wisdom, that when he goes to bed, he will not have rest, because of the way you wisely laid out the facts and spoke with respect. Do this in the spirit of Proverbs 31:26. The Amplified Version puts it this way:

> "She opens her mouth with skilful and godly wisdom and in her tongue is the law of kindness, giving counsel and instruction"

May that be your lot in the name of Jesus. Always ask yourself the question – "will my suggestion make him feel inferior or jeopardise his role?"

Show him respect by your conduct

Ephesians 5:33 says:

> "Nevertheless let each one of you in particular so love his own wife as himself and let the wife see that she respects the husband"

Give to your husband all the respect that you can muster. Respect is something every man thrives on and cannot do without. God has given to every wife the power to turn her man into what God wants them to be and that power is respect. Any man who feels disrespected somehow loses dignity. Therefore, esteem your man and love him. Every man who knows that his wife respects him then go to every length to do whatever his wife wants.

Respect your husband – do not call him names. Show respect in the way you speak to him. It is said that action speaks louder than words. Don't be like the little boy whose dad forced him to sit down quietly in Church as he was causing so much distraction. Finally, when the little boy sat down, he said to his dad: "Dad I am sitting down but in my heart I am standing"! The truth is that some outward expressions may depict a picture of submission but the attitude in the heart may be entirely different.

You must treat your husband with utmost respect. If you are in the habit of showing disrespect to your husband, I urge you to ask God to help you to do something about it. If you have failed to respect your husband in the past pray that the Lord will grant you the grace to begin to respect him. There are over six billion people on this earth but there is no one as unique as your husband.

Understand, ladies – that there are so many women who are struggling to find partners. For such women, the least opportunity they get, they will shower the man with so much attention so as to win his love. In some cultures, it is said of such women, that after the man finishes his meal, they would apparently fetch water in a bowl, and literally take the man's hands, wash them and dry them with a soft towel! In short, they will do everything possible to win a man they know is not receiving his wife's respect. But men also need to bear in mind that such treatment is only short-lived and once such women succeed in taking them away from their wives, with time, they will begin to treat them very badly! The moment they 'capture' their prey, they begin to demand whatever the men gave to their wives, the privileges they had and even more. It is always better for men not to leave their wives because of disrespect, but to help their wives to change.

Talk to him with respect at home and in public

Some women are so used to not submitting that they display that attitude in public without knowing it. They do this in the manner they treat and address their husbands in public. Others also pretend and in public treat their husbands nicely, yet at home it is a completely different story. Such an attitude is hypocritical and ungodly. My prayer is that you will not be found wanting in this area.

Do not share your husband's faults with others

Do not share your husband's faults with others, as this only takes away the confidence of your husband. If there are areas you are concerned about, create the right atmosphere and the right time to share it with him.

Show respect in your speech

Show respect in the way you speak and in what you say to your husband. Refrain from telling him he is useless, or that he is good for nothing – instead, validate him. Don't raise your voice when you are talking to him, as though he is your son. Don't be a brawling woman whose voice can be heard in the next home or in the neighbourhood. "There she goes again!", they will say. That is not the picture of a godly woman. Don't tear down your own home with your brawling. You serve a living God and you must know the secret of taking your hurts and pains to him instead.

Do not tell your husband a former relationship was better than what you have with him. Never do that to your husband. It is very demeaning, and is a sign of total disrespect. **If you really want to be happy in your marriage, you need to be careful what you say.** You see – you cannot speak like that and expect to be happy in your marriage. Part of the lyrics to a children's song goes like this:

> *"....the way to be happy is to make someone happy, and you'll have a little heaven right here"!*

The way to be happy in life, is to make the other person happy. A word to the wise!

Be tactful in dealing with your husband, especially where you are more knowledgeable

Don't use your talent or ability to humiliate him, especially when you are an expert or authority in a particular field.

Act towards him politely when he "knocks on your door"

There is no doubt that wives genuinely get very tired because of all the things they have to juggle. When you feel you are too tired "to perform", politely ask your husband to allow you to have some rest - by so doing, you give him something to hope for and he'll leave you alone for a while! Do not yell at him to leave you alone because you're tired. Gently tell him you are exhausted and would like to sleep until a certain time. I can guarantee that he will not sleep – he will count the hours until it is time! All I am saying is, instead of telling him off, give him something to hope for.... *"Faith is the substance of things hoped for"*! As long as that guy is hoping for something he will not sleep. But mind you, when it is time for him to wake you up – please honour your word.

Be considerate – do not take out your frustrations on your husband

Women are naturally emotional, and because of that, it is very easy for them to pick up hurts and frustrations quite easily. It is possible that sometimes women come home with emotional stress from events that happen at work, and unfortunately, some women take such stress out on their husbands and may moan unnecessarily. Please understand that words cannot be retracted. You may apologise later, but such damage takes quite long to heal.

Never as a wife tell your husband to pack his things and leave the house. It is wrong for a husband to come from work to find his things packed and left at the door with a letter to leave. You cannot keep telling your husband to pack his things and leave the house, at the slightest whim. Remember you stood before the altar and said "to love and to cherish – till death do us part"

Sometimes the frustrations may come from the time of month that it is. If that syndrome tends to affects your emotions at certain times of the month, you need to talk to your husband about it, and at the same time, do your very best to ask God for the grace to overcome such emotional stress and find some natural ways to reduce such tensions. Remember that some men do not understand or accept that there is any such thing, but you can do well to help your husband to understand.

Ask God for a soft heart

Queen Esther in the Bible, spent six months preparing, to ensure that every part of her body that the king would touch would be appealing. Let me submit to you that not only should your outer skin become appealing for your husband, your heart must also become soft for him. May I also reiterate, that not until your heart is softened and submitted to God, you can never be submissive towards your husband. Any hardened heart in marriage is a result of a heart that is hardened towards God.

Ask God for a soft heart as a woman. My experience as a Pastor is that some wives can be quite difficult. Having been a Pastor for about twenty-five years, I have had to settle many marital issues. Sometimes the position of some women is so strong, they do not budge. I pray that you are not that kind of a woman. If you become so angry with your husband that any time you see him you become aggressive, you need to ask God for the grace to change. Of course, it is true that some men do not take up their responsibilities. This angers their wives, and becomes a cause for contention in the home. However, in such extreme examples, my advice is that though difficult, ask for God to give you the grace to respect him, and seek counsel or find the right way of addressing the issue.

Give credence to the things he does well

You can say – "Dear I really appreciate you for all the things you do – you pay the rent and all the bills on time". "You shop for me and the children so that there is always enough food in the house. Thank you for all the things you do. Thank you and God bless you". Tell him things like that. Let him know when he does well. Treat him as a king – treat him with dignity. When you say things like that, he feels respected.How do you think a very responsible and deeply committed family man can leave his home and go after another woman? That woman must be saying and doing things his wife is not doing. I am not justifying that action at all, but you must know that perhaps that woman must be treating the man in a way that encourages him. There is something about respect! I want to assure you that if you give your husband respect, you will never lack fulfilment in your marriage.

Handle money with wisdom – be prudent

One of the ways to show submission is to act wisely in the way you handle money. A man likes to have the assurance that his wife is capable and responsible to manage the funds that are available to them as a family. One thing that amazes me is how women in developing countries manage at times the little money they are given to cater for their family. That is one of the marks of a virtuous woman. We live in a society where we have so much but are always complaining. A wife's ability to manage the little that comes in could make a big difference in the home. Every responsible man desires to provide sufficiently for the home, and during seasons of financial difficulty, he needs a woman who will encourage him, and use her virtuous qualities to help make ends meet.

Ask God to give you the grace to live a contented life. Do you know that some people barely have what you have? There are some who own only the clothes they have on. There are others who only have a pair of sandals, yet with a few clothes and perhaps only a pair of shoes they are in Church every Sunday, praising God. May you develop confidence in God's ability to assist you with your finances and may you put your trust in him instead of material things.

Many people in the diaspora are stacking their wardrobes with the belief that when they return 'home' (meaning their native origin), they will dress well and let people know they have 'arrived'! The irony is that they return to find that the latest fashion is also found in the places they refer to as 'home'. Many of the things some women are stacking in their wardrobes would have become outmoded by the time they return 'home'. A lot of the things we stack ought to be released to those who are less privileged. There needs to be a paradigm shift!

Life is full of seasons

Let your husband know you are content with what you have. Understand that the destinies of people are different. The fact that someone has bought the latest car and your family still uses an old car does not mean that will be your lot forever. Understand that whilst the Australians are sleeping, because they have already enjoyed their period of daytime, the time for Europe would also be coming up. That is how life is. The fact that one family is enjoying today does not mean that your day will not come. Be encouraged - you will soon see the hand of God – your season will surely come!

For many families God is still digging their foundations, so that in the fullness of time, their elevation and promotion will be such that nobody can stop it. God is so good and wise that He will not ruin or compromise His reputation. When the time of your elevation comes, the whole world will see it. Do not elevate yourself before your time. When God himself lifts you, no one can pull you down. Develop confidence in God's ability to assist you with your finances and put your trust in Him, rather than in material things.

Look out for good deals

Understand that it is not always true that everything that has a low price tag is necessarily cheap. The fact that things are on sale does not mean they are cheap or inferior. Many of them are stockpiles which are released again to the shop floor after some time. Look out for good deals, but at the same time, making sure that you are not buying because things are on sale – only be driven by the fact that you **need** those items. May the Lord grant you the grace to be driven by '**need**' rather than '**want**'. Be a wise woman and wife, who knows the difference between "need" and "want"

Use wisdom in the use of credit cards

If you have to use credit cards sometimes, may you be a woman who exercises wisdom in this area. May you not stress your husband out with astronomical credit card bills because you have to buy everything you see. The truth is that many times we do not need them anyway. May I submit to you again that you do not need all those credit cards. In fact, one of the clever ways by which credit card companies get our money is that the moment one company gets hold of you, all the others start writing to you. Do not think they necessarily like you! If care is not taken, you could accrue so much debt that it puts a strain in your relationship with your husband. If you have a problem with impulse buying, you need to ask God to help you overcome this.

Do not force your husband to buy things that he cannot afford

If your husband is doing well within his means, let him know he is doing extremely well. Assure him you recognise his potential and that you will stand with him at every cost to ensure that he reaches his full potential. Understand that your joy is not dependent on the material goods you have but by abiding in Christ. It is only when you abide in Christ that the joy of the Lord becomes your strength.

Often times, we do not take time to find out how other people began in life. We are only interested in what we see of the present. If many of the people who are enjoying life today were to tell their story – the number of cleaning jobs, the early mornings they had to wake up, the number of buses they had to catch to be where they are, you would be amazed. The Bible tells us that comparing ourselves with others is unwise. Do not become envious to the extent that you compare your husband with others. Don't tell him he is good for nothing, because his time will come. He will feel respected if you assure him that you know that your time will come.

Dress like a married woman

The truth about life is that age will catch up with us all. I have discovered lately, that the more I go to the gym, the more I must take it easy. Many times I see young men come to the gym and jump on the treadmill and do it with such ease. I go on the treadmill and I simply walk! I look at the youngsters, and I know clearly that I cannot compete with them. Their heart rate is totally different from mine now. When I see them ran on the treadmill, I could look at them and tell myself how capable I am as well, but that would be unwise because I need to know that age has caught up with me! The truth is that only Jesus Christ is the same yesterday, today and forever. We will all change.

My advice to ladies is that you dress gracefully for your husband – it is unwise for married women to expose parts of their body which are only meant for their husbands. Whichever way we look at it, whether married or not, a woman's dressing gives an impression about her. It is my prayer that as a wife, or a young lady preparing for marriage soon or in the future, you would be mindful of this. Please portray the beauty and dignity God bestows on you as the crown and glory of your husband through your dressing.

Headship is reserved for the man

Headship is reserved for the man, hence ask God to show you any areas that you have assumed headship. If you have deliberately or unconsciously assumed the role of headship in your home as a wife, then begin at once to resolve the situation by gradually transferring the responsibilities he finds most easy to accept. I don't mean you should go to him and throw for instance all the bills and documents at him and say "from today you are the head"! No. What you need to do is to gradually transfer those responsibilities to him. It should be noted, though, that some men leave the sorting of bills to their wives because of the fact that they are better managers of money. That is perfectly okay.

If there is a major goal that I am pursuing, it is to make it to heaven. One day each one of us will stand before God. The choices and decisions we make will determine the crown that we shall receive. If you genuinely believe God and know that Jesus is real, then you would want to make him real in your marriage too. You will simply obey his commandment. Jesus says: *"If you will obey my commandments...".* It is as simple as that. He says that God is the head of Christ, Christ is the head of the man and the man is the head of the woman. If you have assumed the man's leadership role, transfer it to him, and see God move in your marriage.

There are some women who think their word must be final in the home. If this has been your attitude, you must know that you have taken on authority that God has not given to you, and you need to return it to your husband. Do not only see the faults of your husband, but rather pray positively for him. Of course, the truth is that some men are irresponsible. Some are also cowards. When the dog barks they instruct their wives to go to the door and check what is happening. When the bills arrive, they cannot be bothered. Such men are only interested in seeing their wives submit, although they exhibit a lack of leadership. He wants submission in the kitchen and in bed. That is all he understands submission to mean. You can however change things through prayer if that is your situation.

Leadership comes with responsibility.

One of the major responsibilities of every man is to take control of matters in the home. When a man becomes irresponsible and will not pay the bills and the bailiffs are coming to the house, there is something wrong. Even in that situation, you need to pray for him because only the Lord has power to change his heart. Sometimes all you have to do is to go on a retreat as a woman and bring your husband before the Lord. I suggest that when you go on such a retreat, take your Bible and your concordance with you. As you pray, do not only ask the Lord to change your husband, pray that to begin with, the Lord will change you too. Mark in your Bible any passages that talks about submission, the fear of God, respect and the virtuous woman. As you meditate on these Scriptures, ask God to begin to work in your life.

There will never be peace in a home where the woman assumes leadership. The woman will have to do certain things to stay in that position, but because God has not given her that role, it means she will have to take on roles that she is not supposed to. The end result is that she will not be a peace with herself, neither will the husband. The best way to encourage your husband is to be a good follower. If you don't follow he is not a leader. Partial obedience is tantamount to disobedience. The Lord requires your co-operation of full submission.

Beware of Independent spirit

There are so many wives who are "operating" as independent women. That is, they do not do things jointly with their husbands nor behave as married women. They go ahead to embark on ventures before informing their husbands or may not even inform or involve them at all. As a wife, it is unwise to undertake projects or investments without the knowledge or consent of your husband. Work together as a couple. May I counsel you to beware that you are not operating that way. This is never of God and when this kind of thing rears its head in the marriage, it will only lead to frustration, and will steal the joy of the marriage union. Are you an "independent" woman who always makes your husband frustrated? Men naturally don't talk too much so when their wives frustrate them this way, they tend to bottle things up. This is neither healthy for them, nor the marriage. Sometimes you find men who though young in age, would be ageing rapidly. Many times it turns out that their wives are not co-operating in the marriage.

Do not pretend

Some women, in order not to submit, pretend to be "deaf" in the house. No matter what the man says they pretend not to have heard – they ignore their husbands and when this is brought to their attention, they "size" them up from 'the crown of their head to the soles of their feet'. This is usually enough to keep the man quiet. That is not a good spirit. Be ready to co-operate and work with your husband as God intended it to be.

Do not allow your past experiences to stop you from submitting

There are some women, who because of circumstances of the past, feel wounded. Therefore, they make up their minds not to submit to anyone. They are always correcting, criticising, and exerting control. They 'wear the trousers' in the marriage. They wear the trousers to work, to the kitchen and they wear them at night too! They only take them off at their will. Any attempt of the man to put his arms around her in bed will attract a kick. I call that 'scissor kick'. Her way is always right. Unfortunately this attitude has resulted in many men becoming 'spineless'. My prayer is that as a wife, your thirst for righteousness will lead you to submit.

Be careful of manipulation

Do not use your lovely children as a 'bargaining tool' with which to manipulate your husband, as this will only backfire. When you do that, you are giving them a wrong foundation for their own relationships and marriage, and please do not withhold them from their fathers. You will only hurt their emotions and destroy them. It was once reported in the news that a man whose ex-wife refused him access to his children protested by climbing onto the Tower Bridge in London, and stayed there for a number of days. That will not be your portion in Jesus' Name.

Learn the secret of giving thanks to God for your husband

Learn the secret of giving thanks to God for your husband. Begin to tell him how grateful you are to God for his life. He will do even better. The moment you complain as a wife and begin to tell your husband how useless he is, you are speaking against God. You are telling God that His creation is not up to your standard. You are telling God you know better than Him and that if you had power to create, you would have made your husband differently. Honour the man God has given to you. Respect him, pray for his well-being and I can assure you that with time he will become the man that God intends him to be.

As you genuinely thank God for your husband, you will automatically begin to become content, knowing that God will begin to make things a lot better in your marriage. For that reason, do not compare your situation with what others are doing for their wives. You should not compare when you do not know how much that family earns or what investments they have made. Perhaps you cannot afford the luxuries now due to your current income levels. My admonition to you is that do not push your husband to do what he cannot provide. Rather, be thankful to God as you continue in prayer for God's blessings.

Walk in obedience to God

Walking in obedience is a sign of submission. Be determined to obey God's Word irrespective of whether you feel like it or not. If you are struggling with God's command to submit, you need to ask yourself these questions:

- What is it that I am doing that is making me struggle to submit?

- Am I independent?

If you find the biblical principle of obedience in this context difficult, or if you doubt your husband's ability to lead, you must take it to the Lord. As you obey the Lord's commands by submitting, God will deal with your husband directly. Do all you can to accord him that honour, and ask God to give you the enablement to do so. Difficulty in submission to your husband is difficulty in submission to the Lord. The two are related. Say to the Lord, "Father give me grace to obey your command to submit".

When you ask God with a genuine heart, He will grant you the grace to begin to submit, then with your chaste behaviour, purity, holiness and the freedom that comes from within you can help your husband to become the man that God wants him to be.

In an age where the pit of hell has opened its mouth wide to swallow Christian marriages and to destroy homes, my prayer is that your family will stand. May you take the necessary steps to submit to your husband as the Lord commands and your home will become a haven of peace.

Showing respect to an unsaved husband

How does one submit to an unsaved husband? Billy Graham says that "submission is the greatest evangelistic tool believing wives have in winning their unbelieving husbands". Isn't that powerful? This means that as a wife, if your husband is not saved, your attitude in submission can easily win him over to Christ.

We are admonished in Scripture that one does this by living an exemplary Christian life.

"Wives, in the same way be submissive to your husbands so that, if any of them do not believe the word, they may be won over without words by the behaviour of the wives, when they see the purity and reverence of your lives" (1 Peter 3:1-2)

Do not sing insinuating songs to insult him. The man knows already anything you are trying to communicate to him through song, but he cannot help himself. God wants us to *"rescue the perishing"*. If as a wife you go to church, listen to all the good sermons and afterwards you go home to raise a song, the lyrics of which states that "drunkards will go to hell", you are creating a very bad impression. Your husband will tell you he knows he is going to hell and that you will be there too. He will tell you straight away that you are not a Christian because if you were, you would not treat him the way you do. He may even accuse you of being the cause of his drinking.

If you happen to be married to a man who is struggling with the problem of drinking, I pray for God's grace to enable you deal with this situation wisely. Please let your attitude be such that when he comes home in one of his 'high moods', you can gather the courage to treat him well despite the fact that it may be difficult. Take a cool towel, wipe his face, sit him down and tell him because you are praying for him, you know he will overcome drinking. This situation could be very challenging and annoying for the woman.

However, ask God for grace to encourage your husband, pray and break the stronghold of drink over his life and prophesy over him in the name of Jesus – that he will change; that drinking will no longer be his portion and that a day is coming when he will be filled rather with the power of the Holy Ghost. He will begin to show interest in the Gospel and begin to ask questions about Jesus. Know that you are the immediate person God will use to bring him to faith – by your action and speech. It may be very difficult, but once you ask God for His enablement, He will endow you with so much grace that it will amaze you.

May God grant you grace in this area to overcome the enemy if you are facing such a problem.

There is something about respect – it yields positive results. You may be facing a challenge, but I can assure you that with determined patience and respect, there is nothing you cannot achieve. You can win your husband for the Lord.

CHAPTER 3

FULFIL HIS "NO.1" NEED

To treat your husband as a king, note that one of his most important needs, if not the first, is sexual fulfilment. According to many research findings conducted by godly marriage counsellors, it is clear that sexual fulfilment for the man is something wives should not toy with. Hence I refer to it as "No.1" to highlight the fact that for most men, it is a very important and primary need.

A story is told of a lady who went to her Pastor and said:

"Pastor before we married, my husband was so romantic and so affectionate. Now he has changed. When Jim wants sex he wants it now. He does not care how I feel. He has turned into an animal – all he ever thinks about is how he can go to bed with me. At times he makes me feel used like a prostitute, when he refuses to consider how I feel and when I am not ready". She went on to say: "he chases me in the kitchen, bathroom, bedroom, virtually everywhere – I believe he has a demon and needs help". Much to the lady's surprise, the Pastor replied – "Lady, I believe that I have the "demon" too!

Many wives do not understand their husbands' need for sex. Husbands also do not understand their wives' need for affection. Just as the wife's number one need is **affection**, for the man, it is **sex**. If both sides would listen and meet the needs of each other, there would be no problem. William Harley, a marriage consultant, says that "affection is the environment of the marriage while sex is the special event". Men are easily turned on by testosterone. It is stirred up for instance when they see their wives undress.

A man once said to his Pastor that he feels like a fool. "I virtually have to beg her to make love". That should not be so.

Wives need to understand that when a man chooses a woman to be his wife, he promises to remain faithful to her for life. That means he believes his wife to be his only partner till they are parted by death. Before the altar both husband and wife promise the Lord that they will honour, cherish and love each other until they are parted by death. A man makes this commitment because he trusts the wife to be willing and available for this union. It is very important therefore that husband and wife sit down at times to talk about this subject.

For most women, because their number one need is affection, they unknowingly become selfish by denying the man of his number one need. Wives need to be careful to fulfil this need. Unfaithful men unfortunately justify their unfaithfulness in terms of their wives' failure to meet this need. Some women tend to try and make amends when they find out that their husbands are satisfying this need elsewhere, but sometimes it becomes too late.

Many have had their professions go down the drain because of illicit affairs. Some get hooked and are unable to come out of such relationships. It is therefore important for wives to understand that this is an important need. If you had a chance to talk to a man who is hooked on an extra marital relationship, you would discover that the reasons why they are in a second relationship would in a lot of cases, include the fact that their wives do not respect them, or that they are denying them the sexual union. No matter how they may want to explain their action, the Word of God is clear – it is adultery, and should not be named among the people of God. It should not come to that. Hence ensure that as a godly woman, you fulfil this need.

Read about the subject

Unfortunately, many couples enter marriage sexually unprepared. To achieve compatibility sexually, sometimes, one must overcome ignorance by reading widely on the subject. Read as many books as you can, and learn as much as you can on the subject. There are good books by Christian authors on the subject. Couples must also listen during pre-marital counselling sessions, and share their understanding with each other.

Understand how your spouse responds

As you read, also seek to understand how the opposite sex responds. It is said, for instance that men are like electric bulbs! Just seeing their wives undress is enough to get them ready! Women on the other hand are like the 1960's Morphy Richards iron. They take time to heat, and when they heat up, they take time to cool down! For women, showing affection, the right attitude, warmth of personality, kindness, tenderness, and the use of nice words are the virtues that prepare them. Husbands sometimes use harsh words when speaking to their wives and within the next hour or so, would want to go to bed with them. For women, things do not work like that. Hence they see such an attitude to be very insensitive and uncaring. The golden rule of Jesus is that we do unto others what we want them to do unto us.

It is important that both husbands and wives spend time to learn about sex, talk and share on the subject as well as work towards giving each other the sexual fulfilment God has ordained for marriage.

As a wife, you will need to understand and appreciate your king's need for sex. Please co-operate and help him fulfil this need. As you do well to fulfil this need, it will help enhance your marriage.

Cultivate Cleanliness

One Christian marriage counsellor says that the best sex aids ever invented are soap, toothpaste, deodorant and water! Cleanliness is very essential. Engaging in this union with your spouse is an important act of love. Hence it is vital that both partners keep themselves clean and fresh for each other.

Sex within marriage is not dirty – it is a gift from God

Of all God's creation, the only people that God has given the authority and the power to have sex for pleasure and procreation are humans. All other creatures mate for procreation. Within marriage, it is a blessing. Only humans mate for pleasure and to bring forth children. Understand that sex is not dirty – it is to be enjoyed within the context of marriage. However, may I stress that sex outside of marriage is sin as the Bible points out, and has serious consequences.

Sex Unites Couples

Total oneness and union is attained during the act of sex. It solves most problems marriage counsellors cannot solve! As a Pastor, I have come to understand that when settling conflicts between a husband and a wife, one has to be very wise. If the one helping to settle the conflict is a friend, they must be more careful. For if the two of them connect again sexually, that friend will become the third person, and everything that was said and any suggestions they made usually becomes the topic for discussion between the couple, once they resolve their differences.

CHAPTER 4

KEEP YOURSELF ATTRACTIVE

God made women to look beautiful and attractive. Therefore women need to work to maintain this. Every woman must look good and presentable in order to glorify the Lord. It is your responsibility to maintain a clean, neat and attractive, yet modest outlook or appearance for your man. Do not be negligent as it is important for every man to have an attractive wife. Women also need to understand that their body is the dwelling place of God's Spirit (2 Cor 3:9, 16). How one presents oneself is important, because we represent Christ. There is however a caution not only to look attractive on the outside, but more importantly, to let your outward beauty reflect what is within – the virtue of good character and morals and godly values.

> *"Wives, in the same way, be submissive to your husbands so that if any of them do not believe the word, they may be won over without words but by the behaviour of their wives when they see the purity and reverence of your life. That is, your beauty should not come from outward adornment such as braided hair and the*

wearing of gold jewellery and fine clothes. Instead, it should be that of your inner self, the unfading beauty of a quiet and gentle spirit which in the sight of God is very great. (1 Pet 3:1-4)

In other words the most beautiful part of a woman is that hidden person – in the inner man, the unfading beauty that comes out of your spirit – that gentle spirit that comes from within you. The Bible says that these are more precious in the sight of God.

To make your husband feel like a king, look good for him – look like a queen. Every man needs a good-looking wife – therefore, make yourself attractive. There are two ways of making yourself attractive. Firstly, through the beauty that comes from within and secondly in the way that you dress up for him. Both are important. In terms of external attractiveness, I am not suggesting that you look like a size 8 or 10 model; neither should you be drawn into the unrealistic 'airbrushed' images portrayed in magazines. Simply look after yourself by eating well and exercising in order to somehow maintain your figure, and work hard so that you do not look vastly different from the woman he fell in love with and married.

Failing to fix your hair and dressing anyhow is totally unacceptable! Remember that when you look good, your husband feels good. Every man's wish is for their wife to be presentable. The way their wives dress is extremely important to them. Dress with style. Do it with honour, and remember - men are moved by what they see!

How to stay attractive for him

1. Mind your weight and watch what you eat

Balance your intake of calories with the proper amount of exercise like aerobics. Some ladies naturally put on weight easily, and as such need to watch what they eat. It takes discipline to achieve this. Make sure you adhere to the right level of portions on your plate. It is said one of the ways of looking at it is to divide your dinner plate into three parts – ideally, one-third should be carbohydrates (such as pasta, bread, potatoes, rice, etc); another one-third should be your vegetables, and the last one-third your protein.

2. Get a hairstyle that your husband likes

Be mindful that you do not wear just any hair style at all. Be adventurous with your hairstyles! Most importantly, may I admonish you, to get hairstyles that he likes. There have been many contentions in homes because the wives keep doing hairstyles their husbands do not like! If women understand their husband's need for an attractive wife, they would work hard to achieve that goal. Lady, your husband has a good taste so make sure that your hairstyles are the ones that he admires. Remember, you do not have to be attractive to the world, but to him.

3. Dress attractively

Wives need to understand that many of their husbands work with secretaries or female colleagues who probably do well to have time for themselves. It can therefore be off-putting for such a man to come home and be received by a wife who is shabbily dressed, especially when he arrives with some of his colleagues from work. I am not saying wives should over-dress, but be modest and presentable – let it be honourable to the Lord and to your husband.

4. Pay attention to personal hygiene

It is important that you pay attention to personal hygiene. Every part of your body – from your hair to your toes must be well kept. When you have spent time cooking or cleaning, please freshen up and change your clothing for your man.

Inward Beauty versus Outward Beauty

As I close this chapter, may I draw your attention to the fact that **inward beauty complements outward beauty**. The reason I mention this is that I have met women who do well to make themselves beautiful and attractive on the outside, however, their husbands are sadly repulsed by the outward attractiveness, because they lack the beauty of the *"...inner self, the unfading beauty of a quiet and gentle spirit,* as described in 1 Peter 3. What happens is that inward attractiveness makes one even more attractive physically. May your inward beauty compliment your outward attractiveness. Remember, real beauty and attractiveness is "skin deep".

CHAPTER 5

THE IMPORTANCE OF HOME MANAGEMENT AND SUPPORT

Every man expects to get home to find that he receives a welcoming smile from his wife. He also expects his children to be delighted when they see him. Understand that every man needs a peaceful home environment, so please do not prevent him from enjoying that. If you make this a habit, your husband will always look forward to coming home. If for some reason your husband comes home late one evening, the right way is to politely ask why he is coming late, but do not begin to hurl insults at him.

In seeking to meet your husband's need for domestic support, it is important that there is balance in the times spent with the children and with the husband.

When the babies start arriving

Wives must be careful when the children start arriving. Children are the greatest joy that God has given to couples. They will demand a greater domestic responsibility to the extent that the attention you used to give to your husband may change. Some women use the children as an excuse and this can become a problem in many homes. Once you begin to have children, however busy your schedules, make sure you make time for each other. Of course, the focus and attention will shift more to the children. It is even more important to seek such times together if the woman works as well. The couple will need to sit down and discuss how they can find quality time together. For example, occasionally, they could hire the services of a baby sitter for a few hours while the two take time out together.

Many men resent their wives for having more children than was 'planned'. Some even go to the extent of divorcing their wives because they got pregnant again! I do find that rather ridiculous – Such men forget that they are the **'sowers'** of the seed, while their wives are **'carriers'**. The truth is that we will not always understand God's ways, and sometimes He may bless some couples with more children than they expected to have.

Do not make him starve

Fulfilling his domestic need also means planning things in such a way that your husband gets his meals appropriately. Some husbands literally have to literally beg their wives to cook for them. This must not be so. Prepare his favourite meals and ensure dinner is not late all the time. Circumstances are such that at times dinner could be late – that is unavoidable sometimes. However, understandably, it is frustrating when dinner is late all the time! If he prefers his dinner at a certain time, do well to ensure that this is done. For health reasons, some men need to eat by a certain time. If that is so, please be mindful of this and plan the day such that you can do this for him. If both husband and wife have to work, then things have to be worked out appropriately. In my book *"Treating your wife as a queen"*, I admonish men to understand that although managing the home is primarily the woman's responsibility, husbands need to ensure they are working hard to help their wives in the home. There are men who cook occasionally for their families. That is commendable.

Healthy Meals

The health of your family has a lot to do with the meals you prepare for them. Remember – we are what we eat. Therefore pick foods that the body processes easily such as lean protein – fish, chicken, turkey. Include a lot of vegetables such as broccoli, cauliflower, spinach, peppers, greens, etc. Cook healthy meals, avoiding too much processed foods, nicotine, artificial sweeteners, etc. Introduce your family to lots of fruits and vegetables. They are a good source of fibre, magnesium, potassium, calcium and Vitamin C. Instead of giving your family too much puddings or desserts, give them fruit or healthy snacks. I find that when fruits are neatly cut and nicely presented, it becomes very attractive, and the whole family would love to eat it. Sometimes, I have found fresh fruit smoothies very refreshing. If you find that members of your family do not like taking fruit, try converting them into smoothie recipes.

- **Help your family to cut down on their salt intake**. Salt is known to encourage the body to retain water which can cause bloating.

- **Care must be taken in the levels of oil used in our cooking**. Apart from that, there is the need to choose the right oil for cooking. Substitute unhealthy cooking oils with good quality/extra virgin olive oil, for instance.

- **Choose healthy carbohydrates rather than processed foods**. For example, choose brown rice, wild rice, oatmeal, wholemeal and many others in that group. Substitute white bread for wholemeal/seeded bread. The children will soon get used to it!

- **Do whatever it takes to cut junk food from your family's diet and choose water over drinks**

- **Try taking your beverages without sugar**. You can acquire the taste of taking beverages without sugar. To cut down on sugar intake, instead of taking tea first thing in the morning for instance, encourage your family to take water. The good thing about it is that not only does it help to cut down on intake of sugar - it also helps to flush out the body system. Also consider herbal teas, and in addition, green tea, etc, and teas that are good for detoxifying and helpful for the digestive system. Encourage your family to do this for a few weeks, and you will be shocked how the whole body system will begin to change. Some try to substitute artificial sweeteners for sugar without seeking the proper advice. You need to seek advice before you use such sweeteners.

- **Regarding alcohol**, most Christians do not take alcohol anyway, but it is known that just four per-cent volume of alcohol is enough to cause some damage to one's liver. You can imagine what happens when one consumes some of these drinks which have as much as 40 per-cent alcohol content. We really do not need alcohol – what we need is the power of the Holy Spirit.

Create a healthy and positive atmosphere

Note that the subject of domestic support and management goes beyond providing food and ensuring a clean house. It is also about creating an atmosphere in the home within which everyone can flourish and grow. Do well to create a positive atmosphere in your home – characterised by love, peace, warmth and acceptance; a home where honour for each other is upheld.

Colossians 3:12-14 reads:

> *"Therefore as God's chosen people, holy and dearly loved, clothe yourselves with <u>compassion, kindness, humility, gentleness,</u> and <u>patience. Bear with each other</u> and <u>forgive whatever grievances you may have against one another.</u> Forgive as the Lord forgave you. And over all these virtues put on <u>love,</u> which binds them all together in perfect unity"*

Do well to note the highlighted words. You can create a healthy and positive atmosphere with:

- love
- compassion
- kindness
- humility
- gentleness
- patience
- bearing with each other

May God grant you the grace to exercise these virtues in your home.

CHAPTER 6

FIND WAYS TO AFFIRM AND ADMIRE HIM

The other thing that every man needs from his wife is affirmation. Your husband needs you to admire and affirm him. People are attracted to those who affirm them and are repelled by those who belittle or look down on them. Affirmation is one of man's deepest and most important needs. In Ephesians 5:33 the Bible says *"let the wife respect the husband"*. The word **respect** means to 'admire' 'affirm' and 'honour'. Understand that every man needs his wife to affirm him. As a wife, have you ever shown more admiration and appreciation for other men other than your husband - perhaps to a Pastor, a teacher, a counsellor or your doctor, for instance? I have seen many sisters who show more respect to their pastors than their own husbands. It is good to respect your pastor, but please remember that you need to respect and affirm your own husband too.

Showing signs of disrespect to your husband takes away the sense of kingship, and he can easily feel hurt by your esteem for other men. He can develop deep resentment towards all those other people you show respect to. It is important that you note this.

HOW DO I AFFIRM AND ADMIRE HIM?

1. Begin to seek your husband's advice and opinion on decisions

Some women are naturally better than men at decorating the home, however, it is still courteous for the woman to ask her husband's opinion in this regard. Sometimes, ask your husband what he would like to eat. Give him some suggestions on a range of dishes from which he can choose. When you do that, it is a way of telling him that you respect and affirm him and that he is important to you.

2. Do well to meet his requests

Be mindful of some of the requests he makes in passing and try to fulfil them. For example if you know he likes to watch football without interruptions, what you could do for example is to take the children out when his favourite team is playing, so he can enjoy it to the maximum. Most men will greatly appreciate this. This is a non-verbal way of showing him you honour him, and that is affirming.

3. Look for opportunities to praise him

Do not go bragging about your husband, however occasionally when you have the opportunity, especially when you are amongst your friends and they are talking about their husbands, tell them how well your husband treats you. However, you need to do that wisely to avoid creating any envy.

4. **Be ready to listen to his ideas fully**

If you have a tendency of interrupting when he puts forward his ideas, you need to discipline yourself by withholding your reactions until he has finished speaking and until you have had a chance to consider his ideas fully. Learn to be a good listener. That way you encourage him to communicate more and to express his opinion and ideas.

5. **Support and encourage him to achieve his goals**

Help your husband to take steps to achieve his dreams and goals, for instance, regarding projects, further education, etc. If he has been procrastinating, encourage him to take some positive steps towards it. To make your husband feel like a king, let him know that you are prepared to support him in any way you can, to enable him to achieve this. This is something couples should do for each other. Hence he needs to do that for you too.

6. **Be part of the recreation he enjoys**

Your hobbies may differ, but you can work towards it. Some women love shopping, others love the museums, opera, the arts, etc, while 70% of all men love football or some kind of sport. Learn the names of his favourite players. I listened to a tribute once of a young lady who had lost her husband. In that tribute, I was touched when she spoke about her late husband's love for football and that though she never liked football, the husband turned her into a football fan. She went on to say how difficult it would be for her now, to watch her late husband's team play. That is an example of a woman who understands the secret of marriage.

It is also important that the man does well to become acquainted with his wife's hobbies and recreational preferences. Couples who play together and pray together, stay together.

7. Affirm him in non-verbal ways

Communication experts say that 7 per-cent of communication is through verbal communication, and 38 per-cent is expressed through voice tone. To let your husband know you admire him, please be careful not to talk to him with a raised voice, but rather, with a tender, sweet, encouraging and soothing tone. It is also said that 55 per cent of communication is through facial expressions and body movements. You know the saying: "action speaks louder than words". Your body language, actions, attitude and the way you behave towards your husband speaks volumes as to whether you affirm him or not.

8. Be quick to apologise whole-heartedly when wrong

The Bible teaches that as Christians we should not allow the sun to go down on our anger. The sad thing about many men is that they find it difficult to say sorry to their wives when they are wrong. There are also many women who feel too proud to say sorry when they are in the wrong. In seeking forgiveness one should not say: "if you think I was wrong, then I am sorry", or "I am sorry I said that, but you were wrong too"! This presupposes that the person does not accept that they were wrong in the first place. One could say:

- "I am sorry I did that – I did not mean to hurt you"

- "I am sorry – next time I will be more careful", or

- "Dear, I was wrong in what I did and I want to ask you to forgive me"

The latter is precise and straight to the point.

9. Speak with a gentle manner

Don't allow yourself to be driven to the point of losing control, i.e. by screaming, swearing and breaking items around the house. This is usually a sign of someone who craves a deeper and closer relationship with her husband. Often this may be due to the fact that the man spends more time away from home. Hence some women react that way, and is usually a sign of a lack of attention from their husbands. When they do not get this, they bottle things up and with time, react in that manner. If that is your situation, may I admonish you that the best way to get to your husband is to approach him gently, and talk about your need in a much healthier environment.

10. Let him know you are proud of him

Honest admiration is a great motivator for most men. There are some statements he would like to hear over and over again. Tell him some of the things you appreciate about him. For example tell him you liked the way he held your hand in public. He might have done it unconsciously but he will know that it is something you appreciate and so will begin to do it more often. He will become more confident and more likely to try out new ideas aimed at bringing you happiness

Some men complain that their wives are never satisfied, no matter what they do. You need to cultivate the habit of saying things like:

- *"I like that!"*

  When your husband knows that he has brought you pleasure, he will feel appreciated, will become more confident, and will most definitely to try out new ideas.

- *"I don't know how you do it!"*

  With these words you're presenting your husband with "The Husband of the Year" trophy. When you notice that he has done something and done it well, those words will definitely increase his affection for you.

- *"That counts!"*

  These words give recognition that your husband has gone over and above the call of duty in order to show his love for you. When you catch him in the act of doing anything that pleases you, for example, washing the dishes, stirring the stew, making the soup, mopping the kitchen, changing the baby's nappy, ordering dinner – just say – "dear, that counts". That will motivate him to do more to get your praise. It might even become his routine. Let him know you appreciate what he does. A woman who knows how to use words like *"that counts"* or *"I deeply appreciate what you did"* earns a lot of affection from the husband and creates a lot more effort from him, than the one who says things like: *"there is nothing extraordinary about what you did"* or *"this is nothing – I do that all the time"* – A word to the wise is enough!

- *"You always know what I like!"*

  This is an excellent comment. If by any chance your husband buys you something which does not quite appeal to you, you need to find a very nice way of telling him. You should never say things like *"who is this for – is it for your grandmother"?* or *"why don't you ever know what I want".* That should not be your language. What you can do is to politely ask for the receipt, and then suggest that next time, he can go along with you to help you choose an alternative. Once he has an understanding of your taste for that item, he will get it right next time. When he gets you what you like – tell him about it – "You always know what I like".

When a woman tells his man she thinks he is wonderful, it inspires him to achieve more. Affirmation and admiration not only motivates, it also rewards the husband's existing achievements.

While criticism causes men to become defensive, affirmation energises and motivates them. It is said that "behind every successful man is a woman". I believe we can say "behind every successful man is an affirming and admiring woman". Simply put, affirmation enables and energises your husband to be successful . You are the No.1 and immediate person to admire, cherish, affirm, encourage him, and to spur him on to be the best!

HOW CAN I ADMIRE HIM WHEN I FIND HIM IRRITATING SOMETIMES?

My answer to that is simple – look for some good qualities about your husband and begin to talk about those areas. You will not need to look too hard – everyone has good qualities in them. Find it and capitalise on them. You will soon find that this will spur him on to begin to do well in other areas. Do this consistently while praying.

The differences in temperaments can become the cause of "irritation" between couples. For instance, the wife when she goes shopping, may buy two or three of anything, while the man buys a mountain of every item – enough for a month; or the wife could be very meticulous with things, while the husband may be rather haphazard. I believe that despite temperamental differences, with God's help, couples can work on adjusting to build a beautiful relationship.

A WORD TO LADIES PREPARING FOR MARRIAGE

For ladies preparing for marriage soon or in the future, I trust that the principles in this book will be a good foundation towards your preparation for marriage. In addition:

Take counsel as preparation for marriage

Young women preparing for marriage need to understand the importance of attending regular pre-marital counselling sessions before they tie the knot. One also needs to listen to one's parents, especially godly parents. Sadly, some young women refuse godly counsel from their parents, and end up badly, especially when advised against marrying their prospective partners. Many insist, and think that they are old enough to make decisions for themselves. In some instances, when Pastors have intervened, some still go ahead and say they have prayed and fasted enough to know what the Lord is saying to them. They then enter marriage, only to find that the man who perhaps during the early days of courtship seemed like an angel, now shows his real character in the course of time. Then the woman who did not heed their counsel, would now begin to seek it through their parents, pastors or friends.

My advice to young ladies praying towards marriage is to note that not every person who goes to Church is a true Christian. There are crooks in church! Note that when people go to church no search or screening is conducted, so to speak. One does not have to be perfect to go to Church. Therefore, the fact that a guy attends Church does not mean one should accept a proposal for marriage on that basis alone. Hence my admonition to you is that you need to seriously and prayerfully consider any proposal, and at the same time, take counsel from the right people. Marriage is a covenant – a lifetime commitment, therefore it is important to speak to people who will support you in prayer, and also, responsible people who may know your partner. Very sadly, there are dubious people in church, and the moment they get hold of genuine young ladies, they can make life hell for them. Before you know it, you would have stood before the Lord and the congregation, promising to be with him for better and for worse, and so there will be no turning back. Remember, God can also speak to you through your godly parents, your Pastor, and your godly friends and others who may be genuinely looking out for you.

Pray fervently to seek God's will

This is an important life decision, hence one has to seek the Lord in prayer, and only move when one feels confident and convinced at what the Lord is saying. Apart from praying, it is important for proposed couples to watch as well. How do you watch? As much as it is important for you to pray, it is also important for you to open your spiritual eyes and ears. It is also important to open your physical eyes and ears! Listen when your proposed spouse speaks – you can learn a lot about them from the things they say. Sometimes when one is not sure, it may be necessary to postpone the marriage for some time, to seek further the Lord's guidance.

Inter-cultural marriages

I am aware of instances where parents were strongly against their sons or daughters marrying someone from a different country or ethnic group. For some parents, that would be the only reason why they would not give their consent to a marriage. That is rather unfortunate. Scripture tells us that in Christ *"there is no east or west!"* In such situations, the prospective couple need to keep praying, and also seek the counsel and intervention of someone the parents respect.

Prepare physically, emotionally and spiritually

This will be the subject of a subsequent book. However, in a nutshell, it is important that one makes an all-round preparation before one enters marriage.

Prepare Physically

How much have you read about marriage? It is about being organised, being mature and responsible as to be able to get things done. It is   about being disciplined for example in the time you wake up from bed. You need to be able to demonstrate maturity in how you order your life, including making a commitment to learn how one carries out the practical roles of managing a home

Prepare Emotionally

One needs to demonstrate emotional maturity. It is about being able to deal with emotional problems, bitterness, any unforgiveness and emotional pain of the past. It is important that any such issues are dealt with before one enters into marriage.

Prepare Spiritually

You need to be growing spiritually. You need to be a person whose devotion to God is consistent and passionate; a person who is growing in the fruit of the Spirit. It is about being mature enough to discern and make the right choices in life based on Scripture, and also to be spiritually mature enough to choose the right man – i.e. a godly man, rather than to be driven by charm.

Be accountable to someone

You need to be accountable to someone who knows you well who can look at you and push, encourage and challenge you in the right direction, and point out to you areas you need to work on.

As you wait on God for the right man, my prayer is that it will not be long – soon, your path will cross with his, and once you find Mr. Right, I pray that you will also be committed with the principles that will continue to make you the right woman.

If you are already courting, I pray that you will find the principles of this book helpful as you prepare to enter marriage.

CONCLUSION

My prayer is that wives will indeed treat their husbands as kings, and the husbands, their wives as queens. As we do that, I believe the church will be a reflection of homes where marriage is truly what God intends it to be.

Are you the kind of wife your husband can boast about? Are you the kind of virtuous woman that the book of Proverbs Chapter 31 talks about, who combines practical and spiritual wisdom with moral virtues and is marked with an excellent character? Do you understand your husband's journey, and as a helpmeet, help him become the king God ordained him to be? Are you the kind of woman whose attitude and character are such that after being married for some years, instead of ageing, your husband grows younger because he is free of stress, insults and threats? The book of Proverbs describes the worth of such a woman as *"far above rubies"*. You can be that kind of wife that your husband can boast about – an irresistible woman. May you be such a woman - who combines spirituality, practical wisdom and moral virtues and a character that is exemplary; something that comes from within because of your fear of God, and the power of the Holy Spirit that lives in you.

The Lord bless and grant you grace to treat your husband as a king and may you enjoy your marriage as God intends it – for this is your portion – in Jesus' Name.

God bless you.

RECOMMENDED RESOURCES/ BIBLIOGRAPHY

Dobson, James Dr. *Straight Talk to Men.* W. Publishing Book, 1995

Dollar, Creflo Dr & Taffi. *The Successful Family.* Creflo Dollar Ministries, 2002

Hammond, Frank & Ida Mae. *Kingdom Living for the Family.* Impact Books, Inc. 1985

LaHaye, Tim. *I love you, but why are we so different: Making the most of personality differences in your marriage.* Harvest House Publishers, 1991

Lawson, Michael. *The Better Marriage Guide.* Hodder and Stoughton Ltd, 1998

Parrott, Les & Leslie. *When bad things happen to good marriages.* Zondervan Publishing

House, 2001

Pipes, Victor Lee & Jerry. *Family to Family.* North American Mission Board of the Southern Baptist Convention, 1999

Rainey, Dennis. *Ministering to Twenty-First Century Families.* Word Publishing, 2001

Smalley, Greg Dr. *The Marriage you've always dreamed of.* The Smalley Publishing Group, 2005

ABOUT THE AUTHOR

Kingsley Appiagyei, M.A., is the Senior Pastor of Trinity Baptist Church, London, and served as the President of the Baptist Union of Great Britain (May 2009 - May 2010).

He was born in Ghana and trained at Spurgeons' College, UK, completing in 1988 with a BA, and a Masters in Theology with Luther Rice Seminary in Georgia, USA.

After his studies at Spurgeons', the Lord led him to start Trinity Baptist Church, which began in a home in South Norwood with 8 people. Through the Lord's leading Trinity Baptist has experienced tremendous growth, thereby becoming the largest Baptist Church in the UK. For the 23 years he has pastored the Church, Pastor Kingsley has succeeded in providing sound and effective leadership for the Trinity family.

His messages and teaching are centred on the family, integrity, and building godly character as Christians. Through the leading of the Holy Spirit, Pastor Kingsley has led the planting of several other Churches under the Trinity umbrella, in London, other parts of Europe and Ghana.

He is a Pastors' Pastor, and is committed to equipping others to develop their potential, hence is very committed to mentoring emerging leaders and Pastors within the Trinity Baptist Network of Churches and beyond.

Pastor Kingsley has a deep passion for the family and is engaged in activities within Trinity and externally, to foster healthy relationships. This includes a weekly TV programme –

'Family Time' – which seeks to promote family values, as well as issues facing ethnic minorities.

He has led Trinity to begin the Hope Centre Project, in line with his passion and burden for the less privileged in society. Hope Centre caters for orphaned and disadvantaged children, including a child sponsorship programme. The project completed its first phase in 2008 with two childrens' homes and an administration block. The remaining phases comprise a nursery and primary school, secondary school, a well equipped clinic, vocational and IT centre, more homes and a retreat centre.

Married in 1983, Pastor Kingsley and his wife Cynthia, have 4 daughters: Genevieve, Ruth, Esther and Davina.